W9-DAX-749

How To Convince Your Parents You Can...

Care For A Pet Chinchilla

Amie Jane Leavitt

Mitchell Lane

P.O. Box 196
Hockessin, Delaware 19707
Visit us on the web: www.mitchelllane.com
Comments? email us: mitchelllane@mitchelllane.com

Mitchell Lane
PUBLISHERS

Printing   1   2   3   4   5   6   7   8   9

A Robbie Reader/How to Convince Your Parents You Can...

Care for a Kitten	Care for a Pet Mouse
Care for a Pet Bunny	Care for a Pet Parrot
Care for a Pet Chameleon	Care for a Pet Racing Pigeon
Care for a Pet Chimpanzee	Care for a Pet Snake
Care for a Pet Chinchilla	Care for a Pet Sugar Glider
Care for a Pet Ferret	Care for a Pet Tarantula
Care for a Pet Guinea Pig	Care for a Pet Wolfdog
Care for a Pet Hamster	Care for a Potbellied Pig
Care for a Pet Hedgehog	Care for a Puppy
Care for a Pet Horse	Care for a Wild Chincoteague Pony

Library of Congress Cataloging-in-Publication Data
Leavitt, Amie Jane.
  Care for a pet chinchilla / by Amie Jane Leavitt.
    p. cm. — (A robbie reader. How to convince your parents you can...)
  Includes bibliographical references and index.
  ISBN 978-1-58415-799-1 (library bound)
  1. Chinchillas as pets—Juvenile literature. I. Title.
  SF459.C48L43 2010
  636.935'93—dc22
                                                                          2009001121

ABOUT THE AUTHOR: Amie Jane Leavitt is an accomplished author and photographer. She graduated from Brigham Young University as an education major and has since taught in both private and public schools. She is an adventurer who loves to travel in search of interesting story ideas and beautiful places to capture on film. She has written dozens of books for kids, including four others in this series for Mitchell Lane Publishers: *How to Convince Your Parents You Can Care for a Pet Mouse, Tarantula, Sugar Glider,* and *Chimpanzee.* She hopes that young readers will gain an appreciation for animals from all parts of the world after reading these books.

    Special thanks to librarian Annette Draper at Wilson Elementary School in Payson, Utah, and to her pet chinchilla, Chili.

TABLE OF CONTENTS

Chapter One 5
The Softest Fur on Earth

Chapter Two 9
The Fluffy Rodents of the Andes

Chapter Three 15
Will That Be One Chin or Two?

Chapter Four 21
Caring for Your New Chinchilla

Chapter Five 25
To Have or Not to Have?

Find Out More 29
　　Books and Articles 29
　　Works Consulted 29
　　Web Addresses 30
　　Rescues 30
Glossary 31
Index 32

Words in **bold** type can be found in the glossary.

Chinchillas have tiny front paws that they use to pick up food and toys. Their back paws are a little larger, but not much. Each paw has only four toes.

Chapter One

THE SOFTEST FUR ON EARTH

What has the tail of a squirrel, the ears of a mouse, the whiskers of a cat, and the body of a rabbit? Is it a squouse? Is it a cabbit? Nope, it's none of those things. It's a chinchilla!

Chinchillas are not typical pets, and that's exactly why many people like owning them. They like having something that other people do not. Many chinchilla owners like to impress their friends with the things their unusual pet can do. Chinchillas can jump high in the air like a rabbit and even fetch sticks like a dog. They can do stunts like open plastic jars of treats, do backflips over their toys, and perform tap dance routines with their tiny toenails clicking on tin shelves.

Chinchillas are part of a **unique** (yoo-NEEK) group of animals called exotic pets. These pets include many kinds of animals such as hedgehogs, ferrets, tarantulas, iguanas, flying squirrels, and sugar gliders. **Exotic** pets are not the typical pets, and they

Chinchillas are blue-gray to silver-gray. In the wild, this color helps them blend in with their surroundings. Animals that hunt them have trouble seeing them on the rocky ground.

usually come from another part of the world than where the owner lives. Chinchillas come from South America.

There are many reasons to keep a chinchilla as a pet. For one, chinchillas are soft and cuddly. They are so fluffy that they almost look like a big puffy cotton ball. Their fur is the softest and silkiest of any animal's on earth.

Chinchillas generally live for a very long time. If they are properly cared for, they can live as long as 20 years! Compare this with dogs, which usually live only 10 or 12 years, and cats, which live to a maximum

age of 15. For kids who want the same pet throughout their entire growing-up years, the chinchilla's life span is great news.

Another benefit of chinchillas is their sleep schedule. These furry friends are **crepuscular** (kreh-PUS-kyoo-lur), which means they typically wake up around sunset. While this may be a problem for very young children, it is ideal for a school-age kid. While you are in school during the daytime, your chinchilla will be snoozing. Then you can come home, do your homework, and even eat dinner before your pet is awake and ready to play.

funFACTS

Chinchillas are endangered animals. There are very few left in the wild. In the 1800s, people started hunting them for their soft, dense fur, which they'd use to make coats. Millions of chinchillas were killed during that time. They are now a protected animal in South America.

So, do you think you'd like a chinchilla? If so, there's a lot you need to learn about these animals before you can go out and buy one. Turn the page and let's explore the captivating world of chinchillas.

Chinchillas are fun pets for kids of all ages. Even kids as young as two years old will enjoy playing with this friendly animal.

Chapter Two

THE FLUFFY RODENTS OF THE ANDES

Chinchillas are part of a group of animals called **rodents**. This is the largest group of **mammals** on earth. It includes mice, squirrels, chipmunks, prairie dogs, hamsters, guinea pigs, and beavers. All rodents have four front teeth called **incisors** (in-SY-zurs): two on top and two on bottom. People have incisors too, but rodent incisors are different because they keep growing throughout the animal's life. The long front teeth of beavers and squirrels help the animal eat hard parts of plants, like bark and seeds. Rodents constantly have to gnaw or chew on these types of things to keep their teeth worn down. Otherwise, their teeth would be longer than their bodies!

Chinchillas are not native to the United States. They come from the high mountain regions of Peru, Chile, Bolivia, and Argentina in South America. They live in areas that are anywhere from 3,000 to 15,000

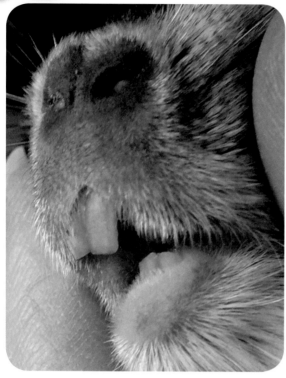

The yellow-orange color of this chinchilla's teeth tells you that the animal is healthy. Owners must watch the length of these teeth, though. Rodents need to have chew toys so that their ever-growing teeth don't get too long. Chinchilla teeth can grow as much as three inches in a year.

feet above sea level! It can get very cold there. It is also extremely dry. Rain does not fall very often in this high mountain desert.

Chinchillas' bodies are well suited for the extreme conditions of the high Andes mountains. First, their fur is very dense. Chinchillas have around 60 strands of fur per **follicle!** Compare this to humans, who have only 1 to 2 strands of hair per follicle. Chinchilla fur is packed together so tightly that their bodies can stay warm even in very cold temperatures.

There are very few bodies of water, like lakes, rivers, and streams, in their native Andes. To get the

water they need to survive, wild chinchillas wake up early in the morning and lick drops of dew that have settled onto plants during the night. They also get some of their water from the foods they eat: cacti and other desert plants, fruit, seeds, small insects, and bird eggs.

In the wild, many small animals have to watch for **predators** (PREH-duh-turs).

Animals that hunt chinchillas are foxes, eagles, and hawks. One way the chinchilla is protected from predators is its color. Its gray-brown fur helps it blend in with the rocks and dry desert where it lives. The fur also has an emergency defense. If an animal bites a chinchilla, the section of fur in the predator's mouth will break free, and the chinchilla can scurry away. The chinchilla also has a stinky defense. Like skunks that spray their enemies with a smelly liquid, chinchillas will spray an attacker with urine.

Some rodents, like the porcupine, prefer living alone, while other rodents, such as mice, live in groups. Chinchillas live in very large groups called

colonies. In a colony, there are as many as 400 or 500 members. The chinchillas dig burrows into the ground to make their homes. These underground tunnels help protect the animals from getting too cold in the winter and too hot in the summer. They also give the chinchillas a safe place to hide from predators.

Baby chinchillas, called kits, are born with fur. This helps protect them from losing too much heat in the cold Andes mountains.

Female chinchillas have babies about twice a year. They stay pregnant for 111 days. Some animals can have many babies at one time, but chinchillas generally have only two or three. Many animals are born with their eyes closed (rabbits, cheetahs, dogs, cats, mice), but chinchillas are born with their eyes open. Chinchillas are also born with a full coat of fur, have a full set of teeth, and can walk an hour after they are born. They drink their mother's milk, but they can also eat solid foods when they are only one week old.

There are two different types of chinchillas. Their scientific names are *Chinchilla laniger* (laa-nih-GAYR) and *Chinchilla brevicaudata* (breh-vee-kaw-DAH-tah). The *laniger* has a longer hairy tail, a smaller body, and

Baby chinchillas can eat solid food at one week old, but they will drink their mother's milk until they are six or eight weeks old.

Kits that are separated from their mother can be bottle fed.

more rounded ears than the *brevicaudata*. Both types have short front legs and longer back legs, with only four toes on each paw.

A large cage with ramps and shelves at different heights is fun for a chinchilla. Boxes with holes for peaking will make the cage feel even more like a chinchilla burrow in the wild.

Chapter Three

WILL THAT BE ONE CHIN OR TWO?

Chinchillas are becoming more popular as pets, so you can buy them in most pet shops. Call your local pet store to see if they have any on hand. When you visit the shop, ask the pet store owner all about chinchillas. Look at a chinchilla and maybe even touch its fur. Pet stores also sell cages, food, and other items that you'll need for your new chinchilla.

Some pet owners don't like buying their chinchillas from pet stores. They prefer getting their chins (short for *chinchillas*) from **breeders**. Breeders often know much more about their animals than pet store clerks do, including whether the animal was a runt and who its parents and grandparents were. Breeders also take care of the chinchillas and handle them from a very young age. This is very important when you're getting a chinchilla. If chins have not been held by humans since they were babies, they will usually not want humans to touch them when they

grow older. Chins who are afraid of humans do not make very good pets.

Although wild chinchillas are gray, chinchillas that have been bred as pets can be other colors, such as white, pink, brown, tan, sapphire blue, violet, and black. Some colors, like pale blue and violet, are rarer than others. Those chinchillas will be the most expensive to buy.

Chinchillas are very social animals. In the wild, they often live with hundreds of other chinchillas. So it's probably not very kind to buy one chinchilla and make it live alone. It's better to get at least two chinchillas so that they can play and keep each other company. Make sure you get all males or all females,

The fur on a chinchilla's ears is a lot different than the fur on its body. It's very short and almost a little scratchy, while the fur on the body is long and very, very soft.

Black and white chinchillas are not found in the wild but may be available from a breeder.

however. A male and a female will mate, and you will end up with more chinchillas than you can handle.

When you choose your chinchilla, look for one that has clean, bright eyes. You'll also want to check the chinchilla's teeth. The incisors should be growing side by side and straight down. The top teeth should not overhang the bottom teeth. And they need to be yellow-orange. A chinchilla's teeth are very important. If they don't grow properly or they get too long, the chinchilla could get sick and die. Another thing to look for in a healthy chinchilla is fur that is soft, thick, and fluffy.

You will need to buy a large cage for your chinchilla. These animals are very active. They like to run, jump, and climb. The bigger the cage you can get for your chinchilla, the better. For one chinchilla, it is

best to get a wire cage that is at least six feet wide, six feet tall, and three feet deep. If you get more than one chinchilla, you will need a cage much larger than this. Make sure the wire in the cage is not coated with plastic or painted. Chinchillas will eat this coating and get sick. Choose a cage that has multiple levels, with shelves and other things for the chin to climb on. You'll also want to buy wheels and other toys for your chin. Make sure the wheels are not made of wire and have no slats or bars—the chinchilla's tail can get stuck in these.

Chinchilla Supplies

food

timothy hay

chew toy

bedding

exercise wheel

bath dust

bath for dust

You'll also need to attach a water container to the side of the cage. Don't get plastic. Chinchillas are constantly gnawing on things to wear down their teeth. It won't be long before they chew right through a plastic water bottle! Get a glass one instead, and hang it on the outside of the cage with only the mouthpiece inside the cage.

A cage with wire on the bottom and a removable pan is the easiest type to clean. You'll need to sprinkle pet bedding that is made for chinchillas in the bottom of the cage. Never use wood shavings for bedding, since some types of wood can be dangerous to chinchillas.

Safe Wood	Unsafe Wood
Apple	Cedar
Aspen	Cherry
Elm	Chestnut
Kiln Dried Pine	Fresh Pine
Manzanita	Tallow
Pear	Cherry Mahogany
Quince	Oak
Willow	Redwood

Even safe types of wood need to be treated before you give them to your chinchilla. It is recommended that you clean any branches with salt and water and then bake them in the oven at 300°F for 30 minutes to kill any bacteria, fungus, or other germs that might be on them.

Chinchillas do love to jump and play, but they also don't mind being held at times. If you don't have your own pet, maybe a friend will let you come over to play with his.

CARING FOR YOUR NEW CHINCHILLA

Caring for chinchillas can be a lot of work. You have to clean their cage and their bedding at least once a week. You need to feed them, supply them with water, and give them gnawing toys. If you get a chinchilla, your parents might have to help you with all the work.

For food, chinchillas need to eat special pellets that have the right amount of **nutrients** (NOO-tree-unts). They also need to eat timothy, a type of grass. Chinchillas can gain weight easily if they eat too much food, so limit their treats to one piece three to four times per week. What treats are okay to feed this animal? Rose hips, raisins, and plain toasted oat cereal are good ideas. If you ever wonder if a treat is good for a chinchilla, be sure to check with your vet first.

Chins need to get plenty of exercise. Every evening, you will need to let them out of their cage to run, jump, and explore. You should confine them to

funFACTS

The name *chinchilla* comes from the Amerindian words meaning "strong silent little one."

one area of the house that you have made chin proof. How do you do this? Make sure there aren't any electrical cords or wires that your chin can chew on. Also, cover your baseboards, or the chinchilla will gnaw on those too. While your chin is out of its cage, you can try to teach it some tricks. Remember that it will take a while for your chin to get used to you, so don't worry if it won't come to you right away.

One of the most important things to know for a pet chinchilla is where to put its cage. Try to imagine what life is like in the Andes: cool, dry weather and peaceful surroundings. You will want to create this same kind of environment in your home. Find a place that is quiet, draft-free, and has low humidity. Put the cage in a well-lit area that is out of direct sunlight and that stays between 55 and 70 degrees F. Remember, your chin is wearing a thick fur coat. It will get heat stroke if it is in a place that is warmer than 70 degrees.

Before you buy a chinchilla, make sure there is a vet in your area who specializes in exotic pets. Not every vet will know how to take care of chinchillas.

Chinchillas can bathe themselves in a litter box that you've filled with the special volcanic dust. Or you can fill a ceramic container with the dust and let your chinchilla roll around inside in its unique bath.

You should take your chin to the vet at least once a year for a checkup.

One of the most interesting things about chinchillas is how they clean themselves. Since they are from a place where there is very little water, they don't use water to bathe. Instead they use dust! Chinchillas roll around in a special volcanic dust that removes oil and moisture from their fur. You can buy this volcanic dust from a pet store. Sprinkle it into a container and let your chinchilla crawl inside. It will roll around and play in the dust and then shake off the excess. Let your chinchilla take a dust bath at least once every two days.

Mrs. Annette Draper is an elementary school librarian. She often brings her pet chinchilla, Chili, to work with her so the students can play with him.

Chapter Five

TO HAVE OR NOT TO HAVE?

Now that you've learned all about chinchillas, you need to decide if this animal is the pet for you. If you're looking for a pet that will just sit in your lap and let you stroke its fur, you should choose something else. A chinchilla will not be happy behaving this way for long.

However, if you want a pet that loves to run and play, then chinchillas may be a good choice. One of their favorite things to do is jump. In fact, they can jump as high as five feet! They are very **acrobatic** (aa-kroh-BAA-tic). They can do backflips and other tricks.

Chinchillas are also fun because you can teach them tricks. They are very smart and will eventually come to you when you call their name. You can teach chinchillas how to fetch a toy, jump over your arm, and roll over on the ground.

Another reason people like having chinchillas for pets is that they don't get fleas in their fur like other

animals do. Their fur is so dense that these pest insects can't live there. Another great thing about chinchillas is that their bodies don't carry an odor. They do not have dander, which causes allergies in some people.

Even though there are many positive things about owning a chinchilla, there are some drawbacks too. You should definitely think about these things before you get one. First, they will make your house very dusty. Your parents may not like this, and you may spend a lot of your spare time dusting your house! Second, chinchillas are known to spray urine out of their cage. Remember, this is something that they do in the wild, so why would they stop just because they are living in your house? To protect your walls and carpet, you will need to cover both with plastic trash bags or a colorful shower curtain. Third, chins are known to be messy. They'll

fun FACTS

The first chinchillas were brought to the United States in 1923 by U.S. engineer Matthew Chapman. He started a breeding program for the animals in California. Nearly all chinchilla pets in the U.S. today come from these 12 wild chinchillas.

Owning a chinchilla is fun for the whole family, but it's also a lot of work. You'll need to make sure you spend time with your pet every single day.

toss their bedding and food out of the cage. Fourth, chinchillas require a lot of time. You will have to spend at least an hour every night with your chinchilla, either playing with it, feeding it, or cleaning its cage. Since chinchillas live for up to 20 years, that's a lot of time to promise to give your new pet. Fifth, this isn't a pet that you'll be able to take care of on your own. Your parents will have to agree to help you with it.

Despite these drawbacks, many people still choose a chinchilla as a pet. In fact, there are over 800,000 households worldwide that own at least one.

Just like children, chinchillas want to have fun! These two animals are getting to celebrate their big day. If you throw a birthday party for your pets, just make sure you give them treats they can eat. Cake isn't one of them!

Will yours be one of them? Talk it over with your parents and discuss the pros and cons. If they say yes, get out there and start looking. There's a furry little friend from the Andes that's just waiting to come home with you!

Books & Articles

Alderton, David. *Chinchillas* (Animal Planet Pet Care Library). Neptune, NJ: TFH Publications, 2007.

Stockwell, Cassidy. "Surprising Species." *Scholastic DynaMath*. April 2007. Vol. 25, Issue 7, pp. 4–5.

Vanderlip, Sharon L. *The Chinchilla Handbook* (Barron's Pet Handbooks). New York: Barron's Educational Series, 2006.

Works Consulted

"An Inescapable Buzz." *Discover*. October 1995, Vol. 16, Issue 10, p. 20.

"Buying a Chinchilla: Things to Consider." Veterinary & Aquatic Services Department, Drs. Foster & Smith, Inc. http://www.peteducation.com/article.cfm?cls=18&cat=1800&articleid=1640

"Chilly Future for Chinchillas?" *Futurist*. Mar/Apr 1993. Vol. 27, Issue 2, p. 6.

Chinchilla Facts. http://www.chinnitude.com/facts.htm

Chinchilla lanigera. http://animaldiversity.ummz.umich.edu/site/accounts/information/Chinchilla_lanigera.html

Chinchilla Planet: "Caring for Your Pet Chinchilla." http://www.chinchillaplanet.com/

"Exotic Pets and Disease." *Pediatrics for Parents*. 2004. Vol. 21, Issue 7, p. 7.

Nash, Holly. "Setting Up a Chinchilla Cage." http://www.peteducation.com/article.cfm?cls=18&cat=1800&articleid=366

Spotorno, Angel E., et al. *"Chinchilla laniger." Mammalian Species.* December 15, 2004. No. 758. pp. 1–9. http://www.science.smith.edu/departments/Biology/ VHAYSSEN/msi/pdf/758_Chinchilla_laniger.pdf

Utah's Hogle Zoo: Long-tailed Chinchilla. https://www. hoglezoo.org/meet_our_animals/animal_finder/Long_ tailed_Chinchilla

Wise Geek: "Do Chinchillas Make Good Pets?" http://www. wisegeek.com/do-chinchillas-make-good-pets.htm

Worthen, Molly. "The Trouble with Pocket Pets." *Time.* June 23, 2003. Vol. 161, Issue 25, p. 25.

Web Addresses

Chinchilla Kids Club
    http://www.chinchillaclub.com/kids/
Chinchillas.org
    http://www.chinchillas.org/
The Chin Information Organization
    http://www.chinformation.org/
Save the Wild Chinchillas
    http://www.wildchinchillas.org/

Rescues

ChinchillaRescue.org
    http://www.chinchillarescue.org/
The Chin Information Organization
    http://www.chinformation.org/rescues.html

GLOSSARY

acrobatic (aa-kroh-BAA-tic)—Being skilled in balance and gymnastic movements like jumping and flipping.

Amerindian (aa-mer-IN-dee-un)—People who were native to South America and lived there before Christopher Columbus arrived.

breeder—Someone who gets animals to make more babies so they can be sold to customers.

crepuscular (kreh-PUS-kyoo-lur)—An animal that becomes active just before the sun sets.

endangered (en-DAYN-jerd)—At risk of becoming extinct.

exotic (ek-ZAH-tik)—Pets from another part of the world.

follicle (FAH-lih-kul)—A tiny depression in skin where hair grows.

incisors (in-SY-zurs)—Teeth meant for cutting or gnawing. In animals, they're the two front teeth on both the top and bottom of the mouth.

mammal—Warm-blooded animal that produces milk for its young.

nutrient (noo-TREE-unt)—One of the parts of food used to provide life and growth.

predators (PREH-duh-turs)—Animals that hunt other animals for food.

rodents—Mammals that have long continuously-growing incisors.

unique (yoo-NEEK)—One of a kind.

INDEX

Andes 9–11, 12, 22
Argentina 9
Bolivia 9
breeders 15, 26
Chapman, Matthew 26
Chile 9
Chili the Chinchilla 24
chinchilla
  and allergies 26
  babies (kits) 12, 15
  cage for 14, 17–19, 21, 22
  colony 12
  defenses 11
  feet of 4, 13
  food 10–11, 18, 21, 27, 28
  fur 5, 6, 10, 11, 12, 16, 17,
    22, 23, 25–26
  healthy 17
  holding a 20, 25
  life span of 6–7, 27
  playing with 20, 21, 24,
    25, 27
  size of 11
  teeth of 9, 10, 17
  tricks 5, 22, 25

water for 10–11, 19, 21
in the wild 6, 7, 10–12,
  14, 16, 26
Chinchilla brevicaudata
  12–13
Chinchilla laniger 12–13
chin-proofing 22
crepuscular 7
Draper, Annette 24
dust bath 18, 23, 26
exotic pets 5–6
follicle 10
mammals 9
Peru 9
pet bedding 18, 19, 27
pet stores 15
rodents 9, 10, 11
shelves 14, 18
treats 21, 28
toys 18, 21
urine 11, 26
vet 21, 22–23
volcanic dust 23
wheels 18
wood, safe and unsafe 19